LOVE ACROSS MILES, DREAMS COME TRUE

LOVE ACROSS MILES, DREAMS COME TRUE

David S. Bell

To order additional copies of this book, contact:
Xlibris Corporation
1-888-795-4274
www.Xlibris.com
Orders@Xlibris.com
38158

CONTENTS

Section 4: Growing in Love 115

Dedicated to the co-author of the greatest love story ever written, my princess Elena

Cover photographs by Hanna Lebedyeva
Graphic concept design by Kristin Bell
Background art from
http://nagietek.herbapol.pl/~darek/3d_ocean/page_03.htm
Special Thanks to Jim at Fiancée Visas
http://www.fianceevisas.net/

SECTION 1

The Love Story

David of Moorpark, California, USA and Elena of Kherson, Ukraine are soon to be David and Elena Bell. After years of searching for a mystical depth of heart and soul within their own countries, they both decided to look beyond their borders. They met online and realized they had found something special, an answer to their prayers, the realization of their dreams. They met in person and confirmed what they realized in emails and letters. Then, because of visa regulations between their two countries, they had to spend much time apart. But their love grew and flourished across the miles. This book is a collection of many of the poems sent from David to Elena during the anxious days awaiting permission from the US Government for Elena to enter the USA and marry.

Together with you

such a beautiful
and loving story can be told
without a single word
just loving gazes
and joyful smiles
the scent of jasmine
and warm candle light
shines on your moist lips
and sparkles with your smile
you sit on my lap
your arms around me
I look into your eyes
to witness the heaven in your soul
the loving in your heart
and my eyes slowly close
as my lips touch yours
my head is light
my heart pounds inside
and I want this kiss to never end
all the nourishment I need
is the taste of you
my hands glide along the silky smoothness
of your shoulders and back
I feel I am flying
on the wings of love
with you above the billowy clouds
where rainbows and dreams meet
and become real

I hug your body closer to mine
and higher we fly
deeper we kiss
and I want this kiss to never end
you are my dream come true
you and I are one
I want to adore you
and praise you
in the candle light
without a word

One Heart

was it the wind
that whispered your name
or did you call to me
from the depths of my soul?
as the wind descends from the heavens
and cools me with its gentle touch
your love surrounds me
flows through me
having no end
no seam between your heart and mine
we are one heart
and one soul
a feeling of the greatest love
encircles us both
no matter how far apart we are
this longing burns inside of me
for your arms to encircle me
and your lips gently upon my lips
then I am complete
so hold me my love
and never let me go
even if tonight
it is only in our dreams
because I am holding you close to me
as I drift into a dream
of you
of us
my love

Perfect

The individual journeys
that you and I had lived
shaped our character
our wisdom
our souls
and even though the world around us
saw as foolish the belief in love
we believed
and we called out
to each other
across the world
because now
the time is perfect
for you and I
to come together
Since the beginning of time
it was destiny
that we be together
and now the time is perfect
and when we look
in each others eyes
we see and feel the heart and soul
that was destined
to be with our own
so natural to be as one
you the key
that has unlocked my heart

and opened it to overflowing
with love for you
a love so perfect
it will blossom and grow
through any test of time
the eternal happiness I feel
within my heart, soul and mind
is perfect
and when I am with you
all is perfect
I love you and miss you so very much

This World

this world
can be such a harsh place
not that the world is bad
just too many people choosing to fear
that want to keep people as unhappy
and as unfulfilled as they
this the background of life
and in the background it can stay
it is disappearing from my view
and from my mind
for I am coming to you
and when we are together
we create our own world
love is all that matters
love is the most important
our love is all around us
and makes dreams come real
our love just gets stronger and stronger
radiant and warm like the sun on a spring day
the mountains and the lakes all respond in beauty
for the greatest beauty
is a soul that believes
a heart that loves
and a mind at peace
keeping the background out
you are my dreamer
my princess
my future wife
reason for living

and I your humble servant
your prince
with the gentleness of true strength
and the strength of true gentleness
we create our world
to the background of beautiful music
the music of our hearts
our voices, our laughter
our quiet sighs of a thousand words
the feelings
the sounds
of love
our new world

Gifts of love

this entire world
is lifted up
with great expressions
of love
of passion
of courage
inspiration touches all
and makes life better for everyone
it is not the warrior
that is most courageous
control is an illusion of mutual consent
dying is easier
living is harder
when most people live as if they were dead
courage
is daring to dream
daring to love
daring to make love real
daring to surrender to each other
to be one
to be who we truly are
and share as one
love does not judge
but delights in the beauty that is real
love is so creative
each day finding new ways
to love
to create
to express
my sweet love, you are the artist

and I your canvas
your love the inspiration
your touch, you lips
the brushes
paint your love upon me
on my lips
on my flesh
give to me your colors, your moods
the fine, the broad brush strokes of your love
the cool, moist, verdant green of your eyes
the hot, fiery red of your hair

This canvas has been long scorched
by a harsh sun
and thirsts for you
for the expression of your love
You will be my flower
and I will be your rain, your sun
I cherish you
I adore you
I will hold you so no cold can harm you
within the warmth of our arms
our love flourishes
we are like the spring
with sweet green leaves
abundant yellow sunflowers
inside
the light always shines
radiant sunlight
mystical moonlight
dreamy starlight
your love makes magic in me
and it is ours to share
and the world
will feel our love
and be lifted up

When I am with you again

Everyday
in every second
I live for the moment
when we will be together again
there is so much love
I can share with you
through words of letters and poems
but I need so much to be with you
to feel you close to me
to look into your eyes
feel you heart and soul
radiate such beautiful light
and tell you all the feelings
in my heart and mind
I need so much to be with you
now and forever
I want you to see once again
my love for you in my eyes
and feel my voice
resonate in your ears
and in your soul
Every time I see your pictures
I smile with complete happiness
and memories of being with you
thinking of the miracles of dreams come true
and that only makes me want you more
I want to share each moment
with beautiful
gorgeous
lovely
playful
and wise
Elena!

Greatest Story

there are so many stories
through the ages
of wonderful fortune
magical miracles
that have touched people's lives
you are the greatest miracle
you are God's most wonderful creation
our love the greatest He has ever made
every day
together
we will make new miracles
our love stronger and stronger
with every day
happier and happier
with every moment
you are my angel
you are my breath
you are my sunshine
I love you so very much

So Happy

You have made me so very happy
happier than I have ever been
far beyond any of the simple pleasures
that I felt as a child
because this happiness overflows
from my heart
to my soul
and through my mind
it as a part of my body
as the blood flowing through me
this happiness is so complete
the happiness of finding the precious jewel
I have sought all my life
for your beauty
of heart, soul, mind and body
are vastly beyond any worldly treasure
you are the most wonderful angel
that heaven has ever created
your love is as timeless as the universe
I wished upon the starry night sky
and you rode a shooting star down to this earth
and this earth is a better place
because you are here
and my heart has been raised to the heavens
because you love me
and our love together
lights our days and nights
I was made for you
and you for me
I need to be close to you
I need to be with you
now and forever

Your Kiss

in your kiss
I taste all the words
that we cannot say
all the amazing feelings
so difficult to express
I share your breath
I share your soul
and my heart beats with excitement
beats with such happiness
your sweet and tender lips on mine
and I am in heaven
with heaven's most beautiful angel
My princess
let me tell you a story
of a great and wonderful love
that grows stronger with every day
and lives on forever
let me tell you, my love
what words cannot express
let me speak to you
with my kiss

Wonderful day

today
is a wonderful day
is a beautiful day
because you love me
my heart
is filled with such joy
filled to overflow
because you love me
each day
is a new discovery
a new adventure
because you love me
my life
is the best it can be
I have the most beautiful wife to be
because you love me
and I love you
more than any man has every loved a woman
and I will love you
more and more
from now
until forever

Dreaming of you

every moment
I dream how different it would be
how much happier I would be
if I was with you
every moment
I dream how beautiful it would be
to share this moment with you
I wonder what you are thinking
I wonder what you are feeling
I wish I could suddenly
jump across this world
and then be standing in front of you
and see the smile on your face
the radiant light in your soul
because you love me
your love makes magic
in every moment

My heart

my heart
it speaks
and shares a love story
so strong, so tender
it whispers
of dreams that kept my soul alive
that now have come real
it sings
of your beautiful and sweet love
it laughs
with a complete happiness
I have never felt before
it cries
because I want so much
to be with you now

Days to come

It will be so wonderful
making me so happy
such a dream come true
to every day
to come home and see your smiling face
feel your embrace
taste your kiss
I dream of our home together
and all we will share
all the love
all the happiness
all the magical moments together
princess and prince
queen and king
Every day I need you more and more
because you have the keys to my heart
my heart, my soul, my life
so many
days to come
discoveries to experience
so much love to share

So beautiful

there are many special
and beautiful gifts in this world
but beauty was redefined
on the day you were born
you all that is beautiful and more
no moist green forest
is more beautiful than your eyes
no fiery pastel sunset
is more beautiful than your hair
no masterpiece of art
is more beautiful than your smile
no experience in life could be more beautiful
than the precious beauty in your heart and soul
you are
the most beautiful woman in the world
the most wonderful woman
that has ever walked this earth
You are my dreams come true
and my remaining dream
to be with you every day for forever!

Destiny

from the beginning of time
before the red sea parted
before the pyramids stood tall
before ancient and mysterious legends
was born the greatest love story of all time
for as early as the creation
of this magnificent planet
you and I were destined to be together
so I praise God that our time has finally come
the age of David and Elena
a love so strong
a happiness so complete
so special
With every loving gaze
every kiss, every touch
we fulfill
our destiny

Speak to me

speak to me
I want to feel your voice
gently caress my ears
sing to me
I want to feel your words
dancing in my mind and in my heart
look into my eyes
and all time will stand still
there is no day
there is no night
there is only you and I
the starlight in your eyes
the sunlight in your heart
you are the center of my universe
you are my next breath
the air of life that nourishes my heart
you are my last breath
for my life is yours
in your hands
and in your heart
and there I live forever

In my dreams

in my dreams
i fly across the starry night
to you
warm and happy in your dream
I whisper in your ear
and you take my hand
we fly over the moonlit valleys
over the tops of snow covered peaks
we smile at our reflection
in a crystal blue lake
and we soar up to the clouds
in the soft billowy puffs of white
we rest
and I sing my song to you
Oh Elena
oh beautiful princess
oh angel that brings heaven to earth
be with me forever
and the earth
the sky will be our playground
every day will be an adventure in love
come with me now and we will write history
forever will you be my beautiful princess
and forever will I be your prince
forever begins with a tender kiss
and never ends

Do anything

I would give everything I have
fight the mightiest foe
climb the highest mountain
just to look into you eyes
I would do anything
swim any ocean
move heaven and earth
just to hear you say "I love you"
You are my everything
the air that I breathe
the water I drink
I need you so very much
without you I am nothing
with you I am complete
with you I am the happiest man that has ever lived!

Wanting you

Every day I think about
being with you again
every hour I dream about
looking into your eyes again
every second I am wanting
to hear your voice
like music in my mind
your laughter
brings happiness to my heart
your smile
gives life to my soul
when we share
a sunset
a song
a meal
a quiet moment
I feel all at once
an exhilarated heart
and a peaceful soul
with a sense of destiny and completeness
you are magic
you are a miracle
you are everything I ever dreamed of
and this moment
just like the one before
I am dreaming
of being with you

Autumn

today may rain
today may shine
but I just want to be with you
it maybe warm
or it maybe cold
but I just want to feel the touch of your hand
Autumn is here
and colors appear everywhere I look
but nothing makes me smile
as much as when you are with me
yesterday fades with the sunset
and tomorrow grows bright with the sunrise
but tonight I sleep
I dream
of being with you, my love
I think of the days together
sharing beautiful discoveries
and I dream of the nights
we dream together
every moment
my thoughts, my feeling
my mind, my heart
are all about you
and being together with you

All you

my sweetheart
my darling
my love
my every happy thought I have ever had
all combined together
my princess
my sweet honey
my precious
my every dream come true
my angel
my future wife
my pride and joy
my miracle
my reason for living
my wonderful
beautiful
special
amazing
awesome
incredible woman of my dreams
My Elena!

I pray

your love is light
like the wings of a butterfly
like the warmth of the sun
tenderness and strength
kindness and caring
clear windows to the soul
and the love comes pouring in
All my life
I prayed to God
that you would be in my life
and now that I found you
I pray
that soon we will be close
I need your smile
I need your love
every moment is a prayer
that I am a moment closer to you
I need you with me
every day and every night
to be my wife
and we will share such precious and happy moments
we will have our wonderful family
all my thoughts
are of you
all my feelings
are of you
all my tomorrows
are for you

Needing you

I need to breath again
to live again
to be with you again
I need to feel my heart
dance with you
I need to feel my soul
soaring in the heavens
I need to feel your hand in mine
I would give everything I have
just to be with you right now
and whisper in your ear
how much I love you

Counting the days

I'm counting down the days
living for the moments
dreaming of the time
when I am with you again
oh I will smile
and be so happy
and feel like I am in heaven
to look into your eyes
to touch you
to kiss your lips
to hold you in my arms
with all the tenderness
the affection
the passion
of this great love
with you I belong
I want and need to be
now and forever more
I love you so much
my beautiful princess

You smile

you smile at me
and the sun rises in my heart
I hear your voice
and I feel like an excited child
I look into your eyes
and I see the greatest love
the most magnificent soul
you put your arms around me
I feel at home
I feel a love to last the ages
Oh Beautiful Princess
my soul needs you
to see you smile
to feel your touch
Oh most amazing woman in the world
it has been so long since we have been together
but the time is approaching
we will be together again
I thank every moment that passes
and brings us a moment closer
I thank God for you
that I am in heaven when I am with
His most beautiful Angel
I thank you for your love
you are my life
you are my everything
and I love you so much!

Storm inside

is that thunder
rumbling through the valley
or is it my heart
for I am thinking of you
is that lightening
flashing across the sky
or am dreaming of looking into your eyes
the earth sings out
and the heavens rejoice
for you and I
are almost together again
I cannot wait
I cannot sleep
I cannot think of anything but you
and I am so very happy

Magic of you

my heart
it beats so strong
it dances inside
because soon
I will be with you
to look into your eyes
and behold your beauty
flesh, mind, heart and soul
everything I dreamed a woman could be
complete woman, magnificent woman
I need to be with you
nourished by your kisses
and embraces
to witness dreams made real
to feel the magic of you
and never be the same again

Precious Gift

Never before have I seen
such a beautiful heart
a heart that knows
and believes
in the meaning of love
a heart that can sense
the most precious love
because every cell
is made of love
And I, so favored by God
so blessed by the heavens
that this magnificent heart loves me
The heart, the woman
the most beautiful of all
more precious than the largest diamond
or the greatest worldly treasure
more beautiful than the greatest work of art
or the morning glow of pastels across the sky
You are the most precious gift to this earth
and I love you
and appreciate you
more and more each day

To share

I belong with you
now and forever
to share our thoughts
to share our dreams
to share a glass of wine
to share our discoveries
to share our quiet times
to share our passion
and pleasures
you are my life
you share my soul
I can hardly wait
for our wedding day
to announce to the world
what we already know
what we already are
one heart
one soul
one

Blessed by God

never before
has such a beautiful angel
such a precious princess
been born of man and woman
or created in the heavens
the earth has never been the same
since she has been born
she is the definition of beauty
the essence of loveliness
And I am so blessed by God
to have her love
to have kissed her lips
and held her in my arms
Blessed, Thankful
I am so in love
and I will love her more and more
with every passing day
In just two weeks
and I am with her again
God really must love me
for me to share the love
of His most beautiful Angel

Heart and soul

playful and loving spirit
sweet and caring soul
heart that loves
so beautiful
so strong
my soul thirsts to be with you again
my heart needs to be close to yours
in the starlight of your eyes
my dreams come true
in your loving embrace
I am the happiest man that has ever been
no sweeter wine than
the taste of your lips
you are all I need
I love you so much my princess

Dance for me

dance for me my love
I adore your beauty in motion
you twirl
and your beautiful hair
rises and falls in the wind
my heart beats with joy
to watch you move to the music in our minds
and my heart almost stops
to see you smile at me
so lovingly
so playfully
you are the focus
of my attention
my love
my desire
you hold my every breath hostage
you are so beautiful
so lovely
so delightful
so sensual
any woman in the world
would be so jealous to see you now
please
dance again for me
and let me adore you
again and again

SECTION 2

Eros and Agape

"Agape" or "brotherly, unconditional love" is said to be the greatest love that would lay down one's life, but in "Eros" or "romantic love" you can lay down your life again and again and again. It is said the only true battles are inside each of us; the battle between our ego and our spiritual nature. The ego wants to doubt, control, to know right now. The spirit seeks to trust, to surrender to our higher feelings and to believe what we cannot see. So Eros and Agape together are the love, the gift from God, that flourishes and grows because two believe and the belief is made real every day. Eros and Agape together are whole. They are the passion that burns to provide the heat to nourish a loving life and the trust to believe in each other and in the love that unites.

Greatest Love

this world
so large
so many people
so many souls
searching
for meaning, for love
every once in a while
maybe as often
as the coming of a comet
the universe creates
a great splendor
which outshines in awesome measure
and is so wonderful, so powerful
God has opened His heart
and created a new star of love
it is our mutual love
the love that lives
in both our hearts
the more we love each other
the more we share
the more we smile and laugh
the more we hold hands and kiss
the world becomes
a brighter place for all
for we have the greatest love of all
and this love goes on forever

Look into your eyes

I look into your eyes
and I see my own soul
for you are the mate of my soul
and your soul
so precious and beautiful
makes me feel so complete
I look into your eyes
and I see love
a love that is gentle
a love that is strong
a love that can withstand any winter
and flourishes in sun or rain
I look into your eyes
I see happiness
a joy that flows through you and I
a joy that fills my heart to overflowing
I look into your eyes
and I see playfulness
a love of life
to work and play in joy
and enjoy each moment
I look into your eyes
and I see my life
my world
my breath
my all
forever will I love you
appreciate you
cherish you
adore you
and together
we will love
as none has loved before

I feel your love

I feel your love
on my flesh
like the afternoon rays
of the summer sun
I am in your warm embrace
and touched by you
I feel your love
in my heart
the happiest moments of my life
are with you
I am full of your love
like the waterfall fills the river
I feel your love
all around me
like a symphony of sweet music
delighted in the sweet melody
and moved by the deep rhythm
I feel your love
everywhere I go
your heart in my heart
our souls are one
everything I see
reminds me of you
every thought I have
is about loving you
I want to run to you
fly to you
any way to be with you
I need you so much my darling
to gaze into your eyes
taste your kisses
and be at home again in your arms

Kiss

I dream of looking into your eyes
worshiping the gentle pools of green
gazing deeper
into your magnificent soul
then slowly close my eyes
my lips draw together and rise up
my face slowly closer to your face
feeling the electric tingle of anticipation
as we come closer
eyes closed tight
my lips know the way
to your moist, tender, delicious lips
my lips join yours
and my head grows light
my arms wrap around you
and bring you closer to me
I taste your lips
breath your breathe
and I just want to kiss you more
my arms, my lips
speak in their own tongue
and tell you, show you
how much I love you
how much I desire you
how much I need you
how much I want you
how much I want this kiss to last forever!

Embrace

eyes to eyes
I reach out my hands
my arms to you
wrap them around you
to feel you breathe
to feel the beat of your heart
to feel the love and desire inside you
together
your fingers gently on my back
one breath
one heart
one body
there is no place
where I end and you begin
there is just us
as one
hold me tighter my love
this is where I need to be

Candlelight

daylight a memory
starlight twinkles in the cool air
in this evening just beginning
a crescent moon smiles
I light the last candle
the flames flicker
taste and tease the air
shadows dance upon the walls
and the light
sparkles in your eyes
your lips, moist and soft
your cheeks glow with the warmth
of the love in your heart
your soft hair lays softly upon your face
and upon the silky flesh of your shoulders
your eyes gaze into mine
your arms reach out for me
one hand touches my face
the other my shoulder
my heart beats strong
quickly
as I feel your moist lips
upon my own
the light is the flames
the heat is our hearts
and the night glows like a mystic sun

I love you

my princess
my queen
amazing woman
I love, cherish and adore
you are everything I ever dreamed of
heart of a poet
soul of an angel
mind of a scholar
body of a goddess
gentle loving nature
playful exciting spirit
nurturing courageous soul
you are one with my heart and soul
and I need so much to be with you
with you I am complete
When I experience the heaven
of being with you
I will try to find the words
the expression of heart and soul
to tell you how much I love you

Arms around you

I do not want a chilly wind
to ever touch you again, my love
I want to wrap my arms around you
and keep you warm
keep you safe
whisper in your ear
how much I love you
and sing you to sleep
with a sweet and tender song
I would watch you dream
smile in your slumbers
and I would thank God
that I love you
and you love me

Kiss the wind

Oh Beautiful Elena
I sent you a kiss
on the east wind
and sent it around the world
to come to you in the sunrise
and touch your lips as you arise
I want to see your face
and light up your heart with the sun
I want to hold you and whisper in your ear
you are so special
you are so precious
you are so loved

Inspire

Oh precious Elena
you inspire me
inspire my thoughts
desire in my heart
joy in my soul
you nourish my soul
and I feel I am complete
because you are now in my life
all my life have I searched for you
and here you are
I look to the heavens
and thank God for you Elena

Special woman

I look into your eyes
windows to the soul
I see so much
I see a playful innocence
the girl that loves to play
to laugh
explore
I see a wisdom
of many lifetimes
knowing, aware, enlightened
I see a loving, nurturing woman
With so much to give
with so much compassion
I see a mind active and bright
creative and intelligent
I see a heart that wants to be loved
by her one and only for all time
I see a beautiful woman
in every way
a unique and wonderful woman
named Elena

Natural beauty

I awoke this morning
to streams of sunshine
flowing down through a gentle mist
it caressed the flower petals with dew
and they opened in pink, white and yellow splendor
the fresh spring leaves swayed in the breeze
and the hummingbirds danced in the air
stopping only to taste each succulent bloom
all this greeted me this morning
and only reminded me of the beauty of you
the sunshine in your heart and soul
the sweet dew of your moist lips
the joyous dance of
the beautiful feelings in your heart
I am thinking of you
and wanting so much to look
in to your radiant green eyes
I lift up my eyes to the heavens
and lift up my love for you
that it may soar over the mountains
oceans and valleys
and find its way into your heart

Lose myself

I live for your love
I starve for your touch
I want to lose myself
looking into your eyes
I want to drown
in your tender moist kisses
I want to feel my heart beat with yours
holding you in my arms

I want to run with you
on the sandy sea shore
and count the stars over the sea
as we lay in each others arms
every beautiful
glorious, happy
romantic, loving
moment I want to share with you
peaceful and placid
pleasurable and passionate
every moment with its own special memory
filled with you

Beautiful creation

could there possibly be
anyone or anything
as beautiful as my princess?
The earth and the changing
orange and yellow leaves
shout "NO!"
The crystal blue waters
in the splendid warm seas
shout "NO!"
The heavens with all the angels
and messengers that streak
across the night sky
shout "NO!"
the sunlight
could not come close
to the brilliant shine
of your hair
fields of colorful flowers
could not come close
to the magic in your eyes
the rolling hills
and winding streams
could not come close
to the lovely curves of your body
I know with my eyes
my heart and my soul
you are the most beautiful
of all
as beautiful
as the love that we share

Fly to you

oh morning light
waking
spreading angels wings
of red and orange
across the east
you call to me
you show the way
to heaven
to my love
give me wings
that I may fly
from whence you rise
across the mountains
the oceans
to the greatest treasure on this planet
my loving, caring
wonderful, wise
sweet, kind and beautiful
Elena
my new life
my new world
is with you
and with you
we share
the greatest love
the greatest happiness
hold me
kiss me
love me
breathe your life into me

with every kiss
with every embrace
we grow closer
I look into your eyes
and delight in your glorious soul
your wonderful heart
and mine with yours
we are one
forever

Happiness and love

smiles
laughter
loving gazes
love
lots of love
so much Love
happiness
uncontainable happiness
you are my dream come true
and more dreams come true
when I am with you
in every waking moment
my dream is to be with you this next moment
to share life
to share love
to share our wishes, hopes and dreams
to look into your eyes
to touch your beautiful hair and face
to wrap my arms around you
to hear you say "I love you"
and taste the sweetness of your lips
I am restlessly awaiting
the time that I am with you again

With you

Today
I awoke anew
the old world
had passed away
and I took my first steps
on a new land
a new shore
the air, so sweet
the light, so bright
in this new life
beauty beyond belief
happiness beyond any I have felt
my spirit soaring
with the spirit of my soul mate
for this is the day
I am with you

Dreams of you

dreams of pastels
painted on the evening sky
reflected in your beautiful eyes
dreams of you
the ocean breeze
playing in your soft and flowing hair
dreams of life
together in heart and soul
filling the other up to overflow
dreams of happiness
we play and enjoy
the pleasure of being with each other
hugs and kisses that never end
dreams of forever
together
loving, sharing
making dreams come true
I want to share every moment with you
and love you more every day
all I want
and all I need is you

Happy with you

I am with you
I see you
I hear you
I touch you
my heart dances with joy
my soul so filled
with my love for you
and your love for me
I am with you
I am so happy
it is Christmas
and Easter
all at once
it is the happiest day of my life
I am so in love with you
you are so very beautiful
you are the best
the most wonderful
you are everything
I have every dreamed of
this day just gets better and better
for I am with you

Being with you

every day
every moment
I dream of being with you
I think of you
and I feel such love in my heart
and this incredible feeling of happiness
when I am with you
I know that my life before
was preparation for being with you
and every day I prepare our home
for our wonderful life together
as husband and wife
father and mother
every day
I want to make our home
more beautiful for you
every day
I want to make myself
more beautiful for you
my beautiful future wife
I was born to love you
and to share a wonderful life with you
and with you in my heart
this wonderful life has begun
I love you so very much my Elena

Calling me home

the smile on your face
the love in your eyes
the sweet sound of your voice
the healing touch of your hand
I need to be with you
and experience you again
when I am with you
I feel all the love
all the life
I have always wanted
and with you
I am so happy
I am home
I hear you calling, my love
calling me home to you
my darling, I am on my way
let's be together
forever

Words of a kiss

in your kiss
I taste all the words
that we cannot say
all the amazing feelings
so difficult to express
I share your breath
I share your soul
and my heart beats with excitement
beats with such happiness
your sweet and tender lips on mine
and I am in heaven
with heaven's most beautiful angel
my princess
let me tell you a story
of a great and wonderful love
that grows stronger with every day
and lives on forever
let me tell you, my love
what words cannot express
let me speak to you
with my kiss

Words that touch

your sweet words
your loving and healing words
are so magical to me
with every letter you write
your love and care
reaches out to embrace me
and I feel you in my heart
lifting me up
giving me hope
by my side through everything I do
I am so happy
and I am so thankful for
your sweet words

Hummingbird

as sure as the sun
rises in the morning
I dream of you every night
You the soft and colorful hummingbird
you gently float into my heart
and in my mind
although the night be dark outside
inside is filled with radiant light
amazing love and happiness
because you are with me
sharing life and love
everywhere we go
is a happy place
because we are there
I hold you in my arms
and want to hold you forever
but as the sleep leaves me
and the hummingbird begins its flight
I want so much
when I open my eyes
to see you there

SECTION 3

"Being" in Love

Heart, mind, body, and soul. I must have written this phrase many times in the last year because each time I write it, a fresh and amazed joy is released of the actual discovery of a love that is so beautiful at all levels. Thank you God for this amazing gift! Elena and I can look into each other's eyes and have a profound conversation without even speaking a word. The complete happiness of resonating with a love on all levels is such an amazing feeling that is difficult to explain, but I am going to keep trying!

Snow another day

Another cloudy
gray and frosty day
the soft powder
falls from the sky
for three days now
everything is painted white
and the delicate flakes stick to the window
so light another candle my love
and I will put another log on the fire
I will get some more Baileys
and then we are going back to bed
no magazines
no TV
no newspapers
just some soft pillows
a heavy blanket
and two loving hearts
so kiss me again
for hours and hours
without end
and each second will feel
like the first kiss
outside its cold
in my arms it is warm
we talk
we laugh
we love
it may snow for another day
and that is OK

The seasons

it is autumn outside
but spring inside my heart
and summer in my soul
inside and out
all so beautiful together
within everything I see
and everything I feel
is you my beautiful princess
you are the colors of autumn
you are the vibrant new life of spring
you are the radiant warmth of summer
you are my yesterday and today
and all my tomorrows
All my life I have been searching for you
and I am complete with my second-half
I need you in my arms
for all time
I need your love inside me
and all around me
I want to drown in your love
only to be revived by your kisses
I love you so very much!!!!!!

All is good

All is good
All is bright
All is warm
All is wonderful
you are sitting on my lap
holding my face in your hands
nose to nose
looking into my eyes
you make me guess
where your next kiss will land
one on my nose
one on my cheek
another on my forehead
and still another on my ear lobe
then a long, loving kiss on my lips
your arms around me
my arms around you
we stop only to share a sip of champagne
and then your long kiss
and I drink of you again
your hands explore my back
my chest and my face
and I wish them well
on their pleasant journey
your kisses stop
only that you may look into my eyes again
and I am
the happiest man in the world!

Every Day

every day
I need to hear your voice
every day
I need to feel your kiss
every day
I need to share laughter and smiles
every day
I need to be with you
This lovely day
my happiness grows
like the storms in the summer sun
for I will soon be with you
the wind rises with your call
speak
and we will make it happen
dream
and we will make it so
together we will live
love, life, family
and share the greatest love
my destiny is to be with you
every day

Home with you

I am so happy, so excited
that I am coming home
coming home to you
home, is wherever I am with you
my soul, my heart
body and spirit
wander without you
this great love
embraces you and I
and with every embrace, every kiss
there is more love in the world
and the world is a more beautiful place
I am coming across the world
the mountains the oceans
to be with you
get ready my love
I'm coming home to you

Share with you

every time I light a candle
I want to watch its light glowing in your eyes
every time I pour a glass of wine
I want to raise the glass and drink with you for us
every time a lift up my arms
I want to touch your face and caress your body
every time I breathe
I want to taste your breath and kiss your luscious lips
every time I speak
I want to tell you how much I love and adore you
every moment that I live
I want to share the moment with you

Keeper of the flame

you are always
the princess of my thoughts
the goddess of my dreams
the keeper of the flame of love
within my heart
you are my purpose
my reason for living
my reason for loving
and all I want to do
is be with you
share with you
spend every second of my life with you
we are one heart
and one soul
and all my being craves to be with you again
let's replace this loving loneliness
with loving togetherness
I cannot wait
to share forever with you

Soon

it has been too long
wandering the desert
these last few months
parched
burned in a merciless heat
But memories of you
the echo of your voice
guide me across the wilderness
and soon I will spread my wings
and fly to you
I will be healed to look into your eyes
nourished by the sweet wine of your kiss
and your body close to mine
will send my blood coursing through me
and fill me with life
with you
I am home
and I alive
and I am so incredibly happy
because I belong with you
and I will be there
soon

Warm

the night is cool
but your toes are warm
we sit
cuddled together
under a blanket of thick comfort
we feel the heat upon our faces
of the fire of crackling pine
the flames dance on the wood
embers rise, twist and twirl
like small prayers of gratitude
lifting up to the heavens
I gently touch the glow of you cheeks
and I study the curves of your face
your delicate ear lobes
your bright and beautiful eyes
my eyes are fixed on your loveliness
and the dancing flames reflected in your eyes
I am the happiest man
for I am holding you
sharing romantic moments
holding you close
and the last thing I see
before I close my eyes
your tender and sweet lips
about to be kissed by my lips
I feel
so
warm

Breathe life

on a warm sandy sea shore
or a cool green fragrant forest
we belong together
you give life to my heart
with your love
you nourish my soul
gazing into you eyes
kiss me my love
and breathe life into me
hold my body close to yours
and my blood flows through my veins
to my heart like waves crashing upon the shore
wherever you touch me
I feel electricity in my flesh
every cell within my body aligns to you
adoring you
worshiping you
praising the eternal beauty of you
I tell you I love you
and then speak to you
with our lips united
deep
moist kisses
speaking in tongues
our adoration and love for each other
I need your love
I need your kisses
I need your touch
I need your body so close to mine
closer
everyday
we are one

Colors and music

tender
sensitive
loving
giving
gentle
passionate
caring
sharing
the colors of my soul
the music of my heart
the gifts I want to give you
completely
all for you
all I am
I give to you
completely open
sharing all that I am
Many spend their life
to accomplish some expertise
I have spent my life
learning how to love
to make the heart and soul loving
so that I have the best gift
to give to you
I love you so completely
with everything I am
I need you so very much
with you I am so loved
with you I am so happy
with you I am so complete
tender
sensitive

loving
giving
gentle
passionate
caring
sharing
the colors of your heart
the music of your soul
together
we make the most beautiful music
we paint the most beautiful colors
I am yours, you are mine

Connected

I love you so much
more than my life
you are my life
we are one heart
one soul
when you are happy
I am happy
when you are sad
I am sad
when you are
in pain
I am in pain
and it is so natural for me
to want to take your pain away
and comfort you
and love you
my greatest comfort
is to be with you
I am so complete
when I am with you
and I am only a part of who I am
when I am without you
I love you so very much
my beautiful
Beautiful
BEAUTIFUL
Princess!
I need you so much
day and night
to be my queen

You are there

in every dream
you are there
I am bathed in your loving gaze
into my eyes
I am blessed by your loving touch
on my flesh
I am complete by your loving soul
so close to mine
I am so happy because I feel the beat of your heart
next to mine
your love is inside me
and all around me
and you beautiful Elena
are warm and safe in my arms
I love you
I need you
and I miss you so much!!!!!!!

So much love

so much love
so much amazing and beautiful love
love that warms my heart and my soul
and fills me up to overflowing
love that gives me incredible happiness
that I have never felt before
and I want this happiness to never end
and go on and on forever
growing every day
happy, fun and exciting days
romantic, passionate and peaceful nights
I need your hands always in my hands
to touch my flesh
touch my soul
when your lips touch mine
the gates of heaven open
and all that is glorious is revealed
and I feel such joy in my heart
you are all I need
and I need you always
In our happy home
with our loving family
sharing every sunrise and sunset
and now I turn off the lights to dream
and I feel you with me
let us dream together

Soul mates

love is all there is
love is all that matters
love was the sound
of the creation of the universe
and in the moment of creation
we were sent hurling into space
to the outer edges of time
and so began the search
through the ages
twin souls searching for each other
to be one
and in this lifetime
we are blessed
with the destiny of finding each other
and together we create a new universe
of love
of happiness
of light
and through us
others will learn to love
for we have the greatest love
the greatest happiness
for all time
every time you kiss me
a star is born
every time you hold me
an angel is born
and this world
becomes closer to heaven

See you smile

I would do anything
to see you smile right now
I would give anything
to look into you eyes
my soul thirsts for you
my heart hungers for you
I want to live and die in your arms
all I am
all my life
all my heart
all my love
for you
my fingers reach out
hoping to caress your lovely hair
as I gaze loving into your eyes
my eyes close and my lips search for your lips
I would do anything
to feel your smile right now
I need you so much

Greatest miracle

there are so many stories
through the ages
of wonderful fortune
magical miracles
that have touched people's lives
you are the greatest miracle
you are God's most wonderful creation
our love the greatest He has ever made
every day
together
we will make new miracles
our love stronger and stronger
with every day
happier and happier
with every day
you are my angel
you are my breath
you are my sunshine
I love you so very much

My sunshine

The sun is not as bright without you
walks seem longer without you
food doesn't taste as good without you
my life is not as happy without you
your smile is my sunshine
your touch is my salvation
your kiss is my nourishment
I need you to live, to breathe
I need to look into your eyes
and feel the power of our love
Yes, you are with me
every day
in every thing I do
but when I am with you
love is magical
life is complete
and you fill me up with amazing happiness
I love you so much
I miss you so much
I need you forever

Kisses

your tender red lips on my lips
your silky hair on my face
your hands upon my shoulders
kiss me
kiss me again
kiss me forever
all I need is you
and the taste of your lips
every moment, every second
I dream about kissing you
holding you
feeling your heart
beating close to mine
I need your soul
and your heart united with mine
it is a beautiful warm day
clear and crisp
and all I want is to hold you
and kiss you over and over again

Join me in my dreams

a beautiful day
and relaxing night
you fall asleep
with a smile on your face
it is time
come with me my love
take my hand and we will sail
over warm crystal blue seas
we will fly over billowy soft clouds
we will watch the shooting stars
maybe keep one in our pocket
we will write our love across the sky
push the edges of imagination
surpass the limits to new adventures
new ways to share
new ways to love
each dream will be the best one ever
keep your eyes closed just a little longer
and rest in my arms
oh, I wish this dream could go on forever
but with the sunrise, we are another day closer
to being together forever!!!

Everywhere with you

forest
city street
sunrise
sunset
every moment
every place
is heaven
when I am with you
the deep green forests
are not half as beautiful
as your lovely green eyes
I want all my life
to be looking into your eyes
touching you
kissing you
holding you in my arms
I belong with you
and you belong with me
together we make magic
and miracles
and I need to be with you
and forever feel the magic of your love

Lights of love

candle light dancing on the walls
Christmas light rainbow twinkles
silver and gold on the tree
reflecting the spectrum of light
the smell of pine, candles
and your perfume fill
the air
cold outside
warm inside
we cuddle beneath our blanket
next to the crackling fire
our romantic movie comes to an end
we toast and sip our champagne
what to do now?
you want to discuss the movie
but your words are spoken with your
tender moist kisses
and your hands caress my face
my shoulders and back
does art imitate life
or life imitate art?
I do not remember the movie being this good
this heavenly
this magical
you speak again
and I do not want you to ever stop

Drought ends

this drought
seemed to last forever
dried in a desert sun
I feel a change
the west wind
cool and moist
brings life again
the wind that fills my sails
and takes me to you
and takes us out to sea
on a journey of love
love is our life
candle lights for stars
on waves of rose petals
you and I
we are one
one breath
one heart
one soul
one
forever more

Beating of my heart

every beat of my heart
sings of my love for you
cries out to the world how much I love you
and calls out to your heart
to be close to my own
with no space between
breathing together
in passionate kisses
we are one heart
sunset to sunrise
and to sunset again
I live for you
I live for your pleasure
I live for our love
on and on
as wave after wave upon the shore
Oh, if you could only be with me now my love!

You are everywhere

In the sunrise I see your face
in the wind I hear your voice
in the rain I feel your touch
in the flowers I see your beauty
in the moonlight I feel your love
every where I look
every where I am
I see you
I feel you
for you are everything to me
and I want to be with you always
all I need is you
hold me my love
kiss me my darling
love me my princess

Rare

more rare than a total eclipse of the sun
more precious than a blue diamond
more rare than twin rainbows
painting the sky together
our love is so special
so deep
so strong
so eternal
we are the twin rainbows
we are one heart
you are my sunshine
you are my beautiful goddess
every day
more and more
I love you
I cherish you
I need you
I adore you
I want you
together in our love
so many dreams have been born
and are nurtured into becoming real
like the many stars in the sky
and the deep blue endless oceans
there is so much happiness
to discover
and make our own

Ode to Elena

bright and beautiful
princess
angel
goddess
answer to my prayers
my dreams come true
loving
playful
sweet and caring
voluptuous
passionate
your eyes
your hair
your sweet and tender lips
your heart
your soul
together we are one
happy
incredibly happy
happiest man in the world
with you I am home
whole
and complete
forever
and ever
my reason to be alive
all that I see
all that I feel
you
You
YOU!

Elena's Song

incredible beauty
my princess
my ballerina
amazing
strength of character
strength of heart
to believe in dreams
when others doubt
and make them come true
to love across the miles
the greatest love that every was
such beautiful eyes
that see real beauty
you are so caring
so giving
so loving
we are love
we are one heart and soul
for we are truly blessed
our destiny
to love each other
and be together
was created in the beginning of time
our love is the strongest
the most sweet and tender
the most passionate
the most giving
the most peaceful
the most happy
our destiny is to love each other
and bring heaven to earth
forever more

My reason

when I look into you eyes
the sun rises in my heart
also the moon and all the stars
and my heart glows like the heavens
I feel your love lift me up
so warm, so beautiful
so tender, so strong
so much happiness
so timeless, so healing
you take me away
to a place where there is only
my love and your love
when I look into you eyes
my heart pounds
my breath stops
and I need your kiss to breathe again
you are my life
my reason and my purpose
I need to be together with you
I live for the moment
we are together again
I live for the day
I breathe again
when I look into your eyes

Future wife

the future
the sunrise on the horizon
is such a beautiful sight to behold
for you will be with me
every day
and every night
you nourish my heart and soul
when I look into your eyes
I can feel the amazing happiness
of your heart close to mine
and holding you in my arms
always
I can feel like we are both flying to heaven
when I kiss your tender lips
always
we can share the exciting times
the new times of discovery
we can share the love and the passion
we can share the quiet and peaceful times
we can share the happiness of sharing life
with our family
always
forever
my future wife
I so much want you to be my wife

Our love

Our Love
is the greatest love
the greatest happiness
the greatest comfort to my soul
so complete, are you
so destined for each other, we are
my heart overflows with emotions
all inspired by you
dreams and thought and feelings
are filled with the magnificence of you
every day, every night
my heart hears your love calling
and I so much need to be with you
looking into your eyes
holding you close
feeling the oneness of you and I
I love you
and I miss you
so very much

Share the love

a life of love
love being the reason
and the rhythm
and the rhyme
days and nights
of love
where love is what matters
hearts open all the way
to share all the great love inside
the more love is given
the more love is there to give
minds at peace
souls complete
for love is first
and always
my dream
my need
to share this
with you forever

SECTION 4

Growing in Love

The more we are together, the more difficult it is to be apart. But the more we grow in our love when we are together, the more we take with us when we are apart. So how I am suppose to work? How I am suppose to sleep? How am I suppose function in any other capacity when our love for each other is so incredibly strong in my mind, heart and soul and I want so much to be with Elena and we are half a world away? Eros and Agape together, in balance. Making every act a prayer for her and knowing that with every moment that passes, we are another moment closer to being together as husband and wife forever.

Colors of Morning

before my eyes open
I sense the morning light
it feels like yellow
it feels like orange
I open my eyes to glorious red
your silky hair upon my pillow
soft and brilliant
kissed by the sun
I half sit up
to watch you sleep
your breathing soft
like the coo of a dove
I love how your nightgown
has slipped down off one shoulder
I want to kiss your beautiful
and tender flesh
with kisses that slide down the side of your throat
and over your tender shoulder and down your arm
but I do not want to wake you
you smile in your sleep
and softly hum as your face nuzzles the pillow
and the white rose petals
I sprinkled on the bed the night before
God has blessed me with such a beautiful angel
you look so beautiful you take my breath away
my eyes joyfully trace
the satin sheet that hugs the contour of your hip
and lays snug against the flesh of your beautiful
thighs

As I gaze in adoration
on the texture of your hair
and the smooth curves of your cheeks
your eyes open
the rich green windows to your soul sparkle
you reach up to put your arms around my neck
and pull my lips down to greet yours
in the most beautiful good morning
my eyes close
all I see
is the colors of love!

In praise of Elena

I love you so very much
and I am so thankful for your love
Every time I look at your pictures
my heart pounds in my chest
your beauty is so amazing
so rare and so precious
the beauty of your soul
radiates through your lovely eyes
and I am hypnotized by a single glance
your face and your hair
so soft, beautiful, alluring
your body so lean and voluptuous
every curve so sexy and lovely
your voice and your laugh
are sweet music to me
they give my heart so much joy
you are my goddess
you are my princess
you are my angel
soon you will be my wife
my mistress
and my best friend
I wish "soon" was today!

I wish I was

I wish I was your shower head
that I may shower you in warmth
and cleansing moisture that caresses your body
I wish I was your shampoo
that I may massage your scalp
and be the foamy bubbles that touch your face
and slide down your shoulders
I wish I was your towel
that I may kiss every drop of water
from your body
I wish I was your brush
that I may glide through
you beautiful red hair
and delight in its silky and radiant
color and texture
I wish I was your lip gloss
that I may all day kiss
your moist and tender lips
But most of all
the highest of all my wishes
I wish I was with you right now
I love you so very much my Elena Bell

Beauty

all I see
in you
is beauty
and grace
a heart that dreams
a mind the believes
and a soul that makes it real
so loving
loving the greatest love
my precious princess
magnificent miracle
sweet, caring
giving, playful
so much happiness
I need you in every second
your are this moment
you are forever
I see all that is you
and all I see
is so very beautiful

You are so beautiful

You are so beautiful
Elena my love
more than the flowers
of a royal garden
more than the ocean
painted in the dawn's first light
more than the forest pines
fresh from a summer rain
more than a diamond
or any rare and precious gem
more than any poem
with words that touch the soul
more than the brightest starry night
with shooting stars across the sky
more than any woman
could ever dream to be
for you are beautiful
in body, heart, spirit and mind
and your beauty is eternal
my love for you
is eternal

Coming soon

I see the day coming soon
love and happiness
beyond imagination
beyond dreams
sharing and togetherness
heart and soul are one
I see a vision so beautiful
my body trembles in anticipation
I see you and I
together
every time I see you
it is with the excitement
of the first time
and more
because I know the heavenly feelings
I feel when I am with you
my heart and soul belong with you
so I am coming home to you
to look into your eyes
hold you close to me
I see the moments
of such incredible happiness
and such beautiful love
I want so much
for these moments to be now

Meet me tonight

As sleep grows heavy in my eyes
I feel you in my heart
all day you have been
right here inside me
but as I lay down
and drift into a dream
you meet me in my dreams
every night in a different way
and a different place
we may be on a sandy beach
or on a boat
at a restaurant
or relaxing in my arms
I need you close to me
and in my dreams we play
and celebrate our love
and I don't want it to end
I wish I could sleep
enjoy you in my dreams
and then wake up in eleven days
to see you there
so I'll kiss your lips
and hold your body close to mine
and share another adventure
in my dreams

Need you forever

every sunrise and sunset
is just a reflection
of the love
the happiness
I feel in my heart when I think of you
the bright daylight
is the radiant glow of my heart
when I am with you
and the mystic moonlight
is your presence, your love
in my dreams
you are my light
you are my life
just as the flower
needs the light
and needs the rain
I need you in every part of my life
I need you in my heart
I need you in my arms
I need you in my dreams
I need you beside me to dream together
time is falling away
and we will be together again
and when I hold you
when I kiss you
time stands still
and we know the timelessness of forever

Waiting

I wish
this day would go so fast
hours become minutes
minute become seconds
seconds become just a blink of an eye
for i want to close my eyes
reach out
open my eyes and see you
I need you so very much
and these days without you have been so hard
oh I wish I could hold you now
feeling the eternal
heavenly happiness
of being with you
and I never want to leave
every second I need you
with all my heart and soul
oh time
PLEASE go faster

To be with you

Oh to be with you again
to breathe as if it was my first breath
to see such incredible beauty
as if for the first time
you are my life
and without you I cannot live
with you
I am living in heaven
embraced in the most greatest love
nourished by your tender kisses
my princess
my angel
my goddess
You give me a life I never had
that I only dreamed could be
and you make all the love
all the happiness
so real

I would fly for miles
to see your smile
I would cross the oceans
to touch your hand
I would go around the world
to hold you in my arms
I would do anything
to look into your eyes
you are my beautiful princess
you are the music in my soul
the love in my heart
and you fill my minds
every day and night
all I want
is to be with you
and never leave

Our world

my happiness
my truth
my reality
my life
is with you
I need so much to be with you
together we create the world
that is our dreams come true
our world that is the vision of our souls
without you life is so distorted
it is empty
it is as if the lights are turned low
and it is hard to see
and people just bump into each other without purpose
with you
my purpose
my life
my love
I am happy
I am complete
I am surrounded and embraced by your love
and the world is a much better place

Prelude to dream

I lay my head down
and hold my pillow tight
I smile
because I know that you love me
I feel in my heart
that you love me
I feel your essence
like you are here with me
just beyond my reach
so I settle down
and sleep
and let you flow into my dreams
there I hold you
I kiss you
I love you
I look into your eyes
I feel your hands upon my face
I am so happy
I want this to go on and on
but then as I wake
I realize that every sunrise
brings me closer to you
and all that matters
is that I am with you
because with you
what was once a dream
is now real

Closer to you

my heart is beating faster
because I am closer to you
all that matters
is our great mutual love
all I need
is to be with you
you are my life
my heart and soul
soon we will be together
in heaven with my angel
soon we will be together
as husband and wife
father and mother
and delight in every second
that we will be together
my greatest dream come true
is our strong mutual love
and in every day of our lives
we will make more dreams come true

Wishing I was home

I wish I was
home for Christmas
home for New Year
home to your open arms everyday
for when I am with you
I am home
home in your heart
in your beautiful soul
look into my eyes my love
and our home is heaven
I need so much
I live for the days
that I am home with you
for always

Magnificent

You are
the greatest love
I have ever felt
the most magnificent beauty
I have ever seen
the most wonderful woman
that has ever walked this earth
you speak, you laugh
and I hear sweet music
sailing through the evergreen forests
all I have to do
is look into your eyes
my heart melts
my thoughts fill with only you
my soul, is so happy
with a union so perfect
formed by the hands of God
you are my angel
everything I have ever dreamed of
everything I need
and soon
I will be living in a miracle
the miracle of being with you!

Wishing

Every wish upon a star
every Christmas dream come true
every good night prayer
has been answered
in heaven's most beautiful miracle
Elena Bell
every moment with you
I fly to the heavens
We are close my love
I feel it
so very close
to being together
I may cry in the evening
that we are not together
but each morning
we are another day closer
and so each day
I make our home ready for you
for us
for our family
forever

Message in the wind

every time
the wind blows through the trees
and leaves quiver in delight
I hear your voice
and my heart beats with joy
every inch of my flesh resonates
to answer your call
that you love me
and I love you
and I need to share
everyday of my life with you
the most profound moments
the simplest pleasure
all moments precious
because we are together
so let me send my love
and my happiness to you
on the wind

Creation

I know how it feels
to feel the mountains grow
to feel the oceans form
to feel the clouds gather in the sky
for you are my sun
and I the earth
and with your love
I am born again
you see all that is beautiful
and make it flourish!
the fields of flowers
the forests of trees
the golden sand on sparkling shore
all for you
all reflections of your beauty
your sweetness and your care
our love is greater than the oceans
the mountains
we are the greatest love story of all

Destiny with you

Many look to the heavens
for some sign
of how to live their lives
some search the sunset
and others seek their answers
among the billowy clouds
I need only look into your eyes
there I see my purpose
my destiny
and such amazing beauty
I see the greatest love
and the most loving heart
I see the lovely soul
that is one with my soul
such memories of incredible joy
and so much longing
to feel it again
I need you my love

Every moment

every moment
every season
every thought
every feeling
all the love in my heart
I want to share with you
every dream
every hope
every rainbow
is the blueprint
of our happy life together
my soul needs to be close to you
share with you each day
hold you close each night
be one with you
heart, mind
soul and body
you are my light
my breath
my truth
my love
now and forever